OUTDOOR SCIENCE EXPERIMENTS

pil

Publications International, Ltd.

Written by Nicole Sulgit and Beth Taylor
Photo styling by Nick LaShure, Ashley Joyce, and Nicole Sulgit
Photography by Christopher Hiltz, Nick LaShure and Nicole Sulgit
Additional images from Shutterstock.com

Brain Games is a registered trademark of Publications International, Ltd.

Louis Weber, CEO
Publications International, Ltd.
8140 Lehigh Avenue
Morton Grove, IL 60053

Permission is never granted for commercial purposes.

ISBN: 978-1-64558-521-3

Manufactured in China.

8 7 6 5 4 3 2 1

SAFETY WARNING

All of the experiments and activities in this book MUST be performed with adult supervision. All projects contain a degree of risk, so carefully read all instructions before you begin and make sure that you have safety materials such as goggles, gloves, etc. Also make sure that you have safety equipment, such as a fire extinguisher and first aid kit, on hand. You are assuming the risk of any injury by conducting these activities and experiments. Publications International, Ltd. will not be liable for any injury or property damage.

Let's get social!

@Publications_International

@PublicationsInternational

@BrainGames.TM

www.pilbooks.com

CONTENTS

INTRODUCTION.................................4

MANY KINDS OF LIFE......................6

NATURE WALK................................8

WHAT PLANTS NEED.....................10

BEAN IN A BAG.............................12

SHOEBOX PLANT..........................14

TREE TRANSPIRATION....................16

COLORFUL FLOWERS......................18

HUMAN USE OF PLANTS................22

PAINTING WITH CHLOROPHYLL.........24

PAINTING WITH BERRIES.................26

SPORES, SEEDS, AND CONES...........28

MAKE YOUR OWN SEEDS.................30

NATURE AND TECHNOLOGY.............31

HOW ANIMALS MOVE.....................32

HOW FISH SWIM..........................34

SWIM BLADDER............................35

HOW BIRDS FLY...........................36

BIRD-WATCHING...........................37

HOW ANIMALS STAY WARM............40

TAKE YOUR TEMPERATURE.................41

BLUBBER GLOVE...........................42

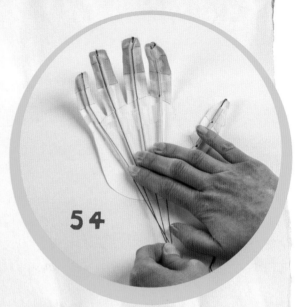

54

WHAT DOES BLUBBER DO?..............44

DNA..46

DNA MODEL.................................48

BREATHING..................................50

YOUR LUNGS.................................51

HOW HANDS WORK........................52

ARTIFICIAL HAND..........................53

FINGERPRINTS..............................56

VISION.......................................58

CORNER OF YOUR EYE....................60

OPTICAL ILLUSION.........................62

BLINKING....................................64

MONITORING THE WORLD................66

WIND VANE..................................68

HOT AIR......................................70

BAROMETER.................................72

SUNDIAL.....................................74

LATITUDE LOCATOR........................76

RAIN GAUGE................................79

16

A plant, a person, a Pomeranian...

What do they have in common?

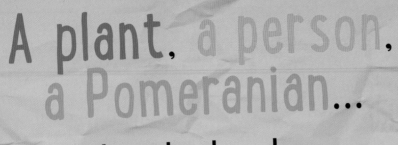

They are all alive! In this book, we look at the varied forms of life that exist on Earth and all around you. How do they work? How do they grow? What do they need to thrive?

Some forms of life, like miniscule bacteria, are simple.

By contrast, the largest living animal, the blue whale, is tremendously complex.

Earth is the only planet in our solar system that houses life. It has water, sunlight, and a magnetic field that protects us from our Sun's radiation.

Living things are greatly affected by Earth's weather and climate. In the final section of this book, we'll look at some ways humans have developed to measure wind, temperature, time, rain, and more.

CELLS

All living things are made of cells. Some tiny organisms have only a single cell. The human body has trillions of cells. Multicellular organisms like humans and animals have many different kinds of cells that perform different functions. For example, humans have white blood cells that help their immune system, and red blood cells that carry oxygen throughout the body.

MANY KINDS OF LIFE

The study of life on earth is called biology. Biology has many branches. Zoologists study animals, while microbiologists study tiny organisms. Geneticists study genes and how animals and other living things pass on traits to their children.

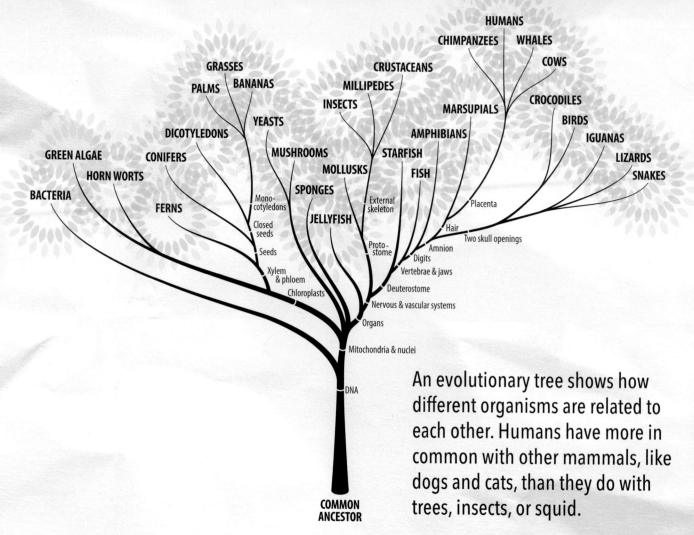

An evolutionary tree shows how different organisms are related to each other. Humans have more in common with other mammals, like dogs and cats, than they do with trees, insects, or squid.

Animals can be vertebrates or invertebrates. Vertebrates like fish, lizards, birds, and humans, have backbones. Invertebrates like insects, octopuses, and sponges do not.

CLASSIFICATION OF ANIMALS

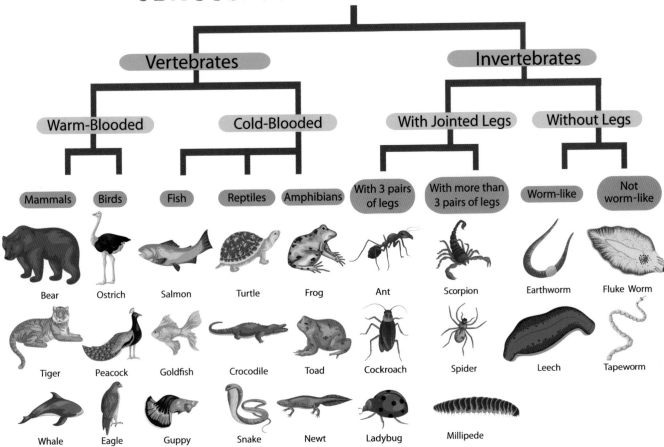

Insects are some of the most diverse animals on Earth. There are many different kinds of insects. And there may be as many as 10 quintillion individual insects alive right now!

The fossil record shows that plants existed on land at least 420 million years ago. Some scientists think they moved from water to land even earlier than that.

NATURE WALK

How many different kinds of living things can you see in a 20-minute walk?

MATERIALS

- Pen or pencil
- Notebook
- Colored pencils or crayons (optional)
- Camera (optional)

Spend 20 minutes outdoors–in your neighborhood, in a nearby park, or just in your backyard. Take notes in your notebook of all the kinds of life you see. If you don't know the name of a bug, bird, or plant, then describe it, draw it in your notebook, or snap a photograph. You can go as a family, and see who spots the most living things!

HOW MANY...

INSECTS?
FLOWERS?
BUSHES?
WEEDS?

TREES?
BIRDS?
PEOPLE?
PETS?

Do you hear any animals that you do not see? For example, you might hear a cicada humming, a frog croaking, or a bird chirping, even if you do not spot it.

SAFETY NOTES

1. If you are hiking in a place with ticks, wear a long-sleeved shirt and tuck your pants into your boots. Check your backpack and clothes when you get home.

2. Be careful of poison ivy and its relatives.

WHAT PLANTS NEED

Humans and other animals eat food, which gives them energy that they use to function. Plants make their own food through a process called photosynthesis.

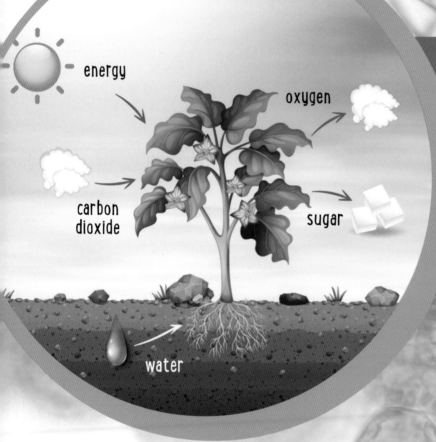

energy

oxygen

carbon dioxide

sugar

water

THREE NEEDS

Plants take in sunlight, water, and a gas called carbon dioxide. In the process of photosynthesis, they transform these into a sugar called glucose that they use for energy, as well as oxygen. Plants provide a lot of the oxygen in our air that humans need to breathe!

WHY PLANTS ARE GREEN

The green color in many plants is due to a pigment called chlorophyll. Without chlorophyll, plants could not absorb sunlight.

WHY DO LEAVES CHANGE COLORS?

In fall, trees stop making food. The level of chlorophyll in their leaves lessens. As it does, we can see the other pigments that were hidden by the chlorophyll. During the winter, the tree stores its nutrients in its roots.

Some simple plants like mosses are non-vascular, and do not have specialized tissues.

VASCULAR PLANTS

Most plants, including all flowering plants, have specific types of tissues that help them move water and nutrients throughout the plant. A tissue called phloem transports sugars, while xylem transports water.

LOVING THE SUN

When a living thing seeks out light, scientists call it "phototropic." In some plants, like tulips, phototropism is very noticeable. On pages 14–15, we'll set up an experiment that shows phototropism in action.

BEAN IN A BAG

How long does it take for a bean to grow? What does it need to grow into a plant?

MATERIALS

- Dried beans*
- Paper towel
- Plastic baggie

* We used pinto beans, but you can use any dried bean you have available, including black beans, lentil beans, navy beans, or mung beans.

Step 1

Fold a paper towel into quarters. Wet the paper towel, then squeeze out extra water. Place it in a plastic baggie.

Step 2

Place a bean or beans into the bag, on top of the towel. Leave the plastic bag unsealed so air can get into it. Place the bag somewhere where the beans can get light.

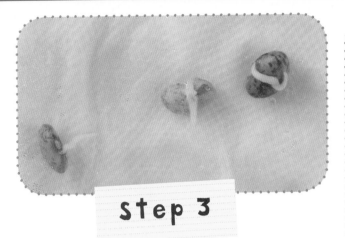

step 3

After a few days, your beans will begin to sprout! In this photograph, the beans have been in the bag for four days.

step 4

Once the beans begin to sprout, they grow quickly. These beans have been in the bag for one week.

step 5

You can transfer your beans to a small container of soil. This container has about 8 bean sprouts. Soil will help your bean sprouts grow even faster.

QUICK GROWTH

When you think of a seed, you might think of sunflower seeds or pumpkin seeds. But the beans you eat on a burrito are seeds too! Seeds contain all the nutrients a plant needs for growth. Once you add water and light, you're on your way. Here are some further experiments to try:

- What kind of bean sprouts fastest? Grow a few bean varieties, making sure they're grown in the same conditions in terms of water, light, space, and air.

- How does light affect growth? Put one bean in a sunny window, another in a shady area, and another in a closet and see how light conditions affect growth.

SHOEBOX PLANT

Do you like mazes? Create a maze for your bean sprout plant and see how well it grows.

MATERIALS

- Bean sprout(s) in small pot with soil
- Empty shoebox
- Two sturdy card pieces
- Scissors
- Ruler
- Tape

step 1

Plant a young bean sprout in a small container with soil. Decorate your shoebox if you'd like.

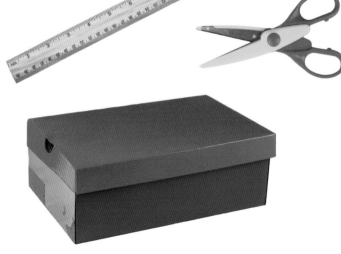

step 2

Cut a hole in the top of the shoebox.

Step 3 Measure the width of the shoebox with your ruler. Cut a piece of sturdy card into a rectangular shape so that it is slightly wider than the shoebox. Cut a window on one side of the card. Fold the edges of the card to make flaps, place the card inside the shoebox, and tape the flaps to the box.

Step 4

Cut another piece of card and place it in the box. The window in the card should be on the opposite side.

Step 5

Place your plant inside the box. Close the lid on the box and place it in a location with light.

Step 6

Check your box every few days. Water the plant if the soil is dry.

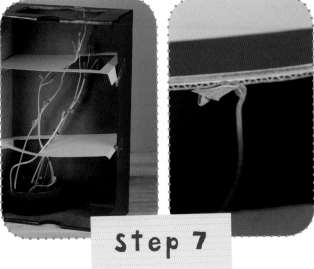

Step 7

How long does it take for your plant to reach the top of the box?

TREE TRANSPIRATION

A tree's roots gather water, which moves up the plant to its leaves. Small pores on the leaf release water to the air.

MATERIALS

- Large clear bag
- Tape
- Scissors
- Rock
- Tree

step 1

Drop the rock in the bag, then place the bag over as many leaves as possible.

Step 2

Tape the bag to hold it in place.

Step 3

The rock weighs down the bag, allowing the water that collects to drip down.

Step 4

Leave the bag for 24 hours. If you check occasionally, you will see water droplets begin to bead on the bag's surface.

Step 5

Cut a corner off and collect water. Don't drink the water and make sure to remove the bag from the tree!

COLORFUL FLOWERS

Can a white flower become green or red or blue? It can, with a little food coloring, water, and time.

MATERIALS

- White flowers
- Food coloring
- Glasses or vases
- Water
- Scissors
- Tape

Step 1

Decide what kind of flower to use. We ran our experiments with carnations, chrysanthemums, and daisies.

Step 2

Cut the stem to the size of your vase or glass. Strip away any excess leaves.

Step 3

Add a few drops of food coloring to the water.

Step 4

Add your flower to the water and set it someplace where it will get light.

Step 5

Try different flowers in different colors! For extra fun, carefully cut a stem into two and place each half of the stem into a glass with a different color. *What do you think will happen to that flower? Do you think the colors will combine, resulting in a purple flower? Or do you think you'll end up with a flower that is half red and half blue?*

Step 6

If the flower has a hard time staying upright, use tape to secure it.

It will take several hours at a minimum to begin changing colors. For best results leave the flower in the glass for several days.

The flower with the split stem will begin to show two different colors. The half with the stem in blue water will turn blue, while the half with the stem in red water will turn red.

HOW DOES IT WORK?

A plant's stem carries water and nutrients to the rest of the plant. The colorful water slowly travels up the stem to change the color of the flower's petals through a process called capillary action. If you tried a variety of flowers, which flower changed colors fastest? Which colors worked best?

Florists dye flowers with several different methods, including the absorption method. They also use floral spray paint. Blue roses, for example, do not occur in nature. While some blue-ish rose variations have been created via genetic engineering, many blue roses are simply white roses that have been dyed blue.

You may see flowers with metallic tinges or glitter added to them for holidays such as New Year's Day or St. Patrick's Day. You may be able to find spray paint that can be used safely on flowers at a local craft store.

HUMAN USE OF PLANTS

If you think about how we use plants everyday, you probably think of food first. But plants and their byproducts are used throughout our homes.

Plants have been used as medicine. Willow bark contains salicin, which can be transformed into salicylic acid, used in aspirin.

Plants are used to make fibers used in clothing.

Trees are used to make both furniture and paper.

PLANTS AND PIGMENTS

Plants, along with other natural materials, have been used to dye fabrics or make pigment for paints. The spice turmeric, for example, is used for orange dye.

Despite its expensive cost, saffron has been used not only to spice food but to dye fabric.

The madder plant produces red and pink pigments. Traditionally, the roots of the plant were dried in the sun and then pounded to produce a powder.

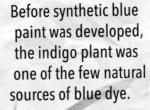

Before synthetic blue paint was developed, the indigo plant was one of the few natural sources of blue dye.

PAINTING WITH CHLOROPHYLL

Spinach is great for your health, filled with nutrients. In a pinch, it can also be used when you need green pigment.

MATERIALS

- Spinach
- Metal spoon
- Paper

Step 1

Place the spinach on your paper where you would like the green to show up.

Step 2

Fold the paper in half, over the spinach. Press the paper with a spoon to release the green pigment in it, the chlorophyll that gives spinach its green color. It leaves a green residue on the page.

Step 3

For a further release of green pigment, you can also crumple up a bunch of spinach in your hands and rub it against the paper.

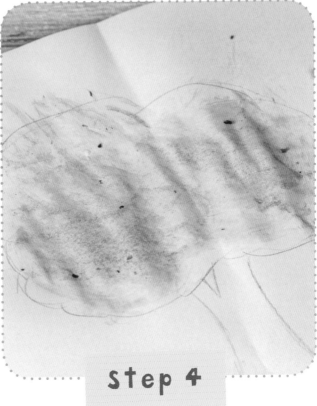

Step 4

Voilà, you've added green to your painting!

PAINTING WITH
BERRIES

Berries provide natural red or purple pigments.

MATERIALS

- Blackberries, raspberries, or both. You can try other types of berries as well.
- A bowl for each kind of berry you're using
- A bowl for eggs
- Egg(s)
- Paper
- Paintbrush(es)
- A strainer
- A fork and a spoon
- Paper towels

step 1

Place the berries you're going to use in the strainer, above a bowl of about the same size.

step 2

Mash the raspberries with the fork.

step 3

Colorful juice falls into the bowl.

step 4

For extra shine, crack an egg into a separate bowl.

step 5

Mix the egg in with your paint.

Step 6

Gather your paintbrush and paper. This can be messy and the paint can soak through the paper, so placing a paper towel underneath your paper is recommended on fabric surfaces or ones that are difficult to wipe down.

step 7

Start painting!

Raspberry juice provides a lighter red pigment.

SPORES, SEEDS, AND CONES

You grew a bean plant from a seed. How do plants reproduce in nature?

SPORES

Some more primitive plants, like ferns and mosses, produce through spores. Spores develop on the plant. Under certain conditions—like warm, dry air—the spores are expelled from the plant and drift on the wind until they land elsewhere. If the spores land in a moist, shady place, the spore may go through a process where a new plant can grow. Because the conditions need to be just right for growth, a lot of spores don't become new plants.

CONES

Conifers reproduce using their cones. Each plant has two kinds of cones, male and female. The male cone produces pollen, which the wind carries away. If some of the pollen reaches a female cone, it creates a seed. Eventually, the seed is carried away by the wind to land where it may grow into a new plant.

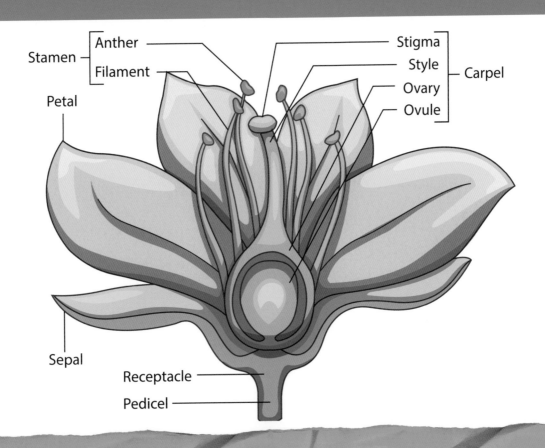

Stamen — Anther
Filament
Petal
Sepal
Receptacle
Pedicel
Stigma
Style — Carpel
Ovary
Ovule

FLOWERING PLANTS AND SEEDS

Flowering plants reproduce through seeds. Flowering plants have parts that both make and receive pollen. An animal such as a hummingbird or an insect such as a bee picks up a grain of pollen from a plant's anther. If it carries it to the stigma of that plant or another plant of the same type, the plant may go through a process that leads to a new seed growing.

A bean plant is an angiosperm—a flowering plant.

MAKE YOUR OWN SEEDS

In autumn, maple trees release a "samara" that carries the seed far from the tree. You might know it as a "helicopter" or "whirligig." You can throw them up in the air and watch them spin to the ground! Make your own samara with construction paper.

MATERIALS

- Construction or tissue paper
- Scissors
- Glue
- Seeds such as sunflower seeds or raisins
- String (optional)

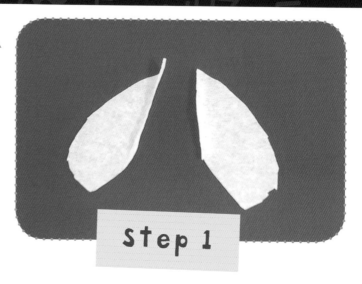

Step 1

Cut out two identical wing shapes for your samara from construction paper or tissue paper.

Step 3

Throw your samara in the air and see if it spins to the ground! You can also create a samara with two wings and join it with string.

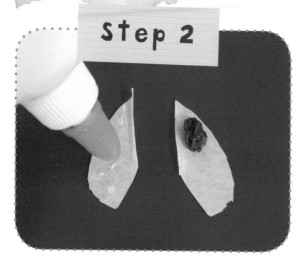

Step 2

Place a seed at one end of one wing shape. With small dabs of glue, glue the two wing shapes together with the seed at one end.

NATURE AND TECHNOLOGY

Do you have a shoe with velcro straps? Velcro was created by a Swiss engineer named George de Mestral in the 1940s. He was inspired by burrs that attached to his clothing and his dog's fur when he went hiking.

Burrs protect a plant. Because they attach to objects and are carried along, they are also a form of seed dispersal.

Have you ever bought seedless grapes? One way to grow a plant is to take a cutting, a piece from an existing plant such as its root, and put it somewhere where it can grow. The new plant is basically a clone of the existing plant.

HOW ANIMALS MOVE

There are dozens of words for how animals move. Some soar, while others wriggle. Some crawl, while others hop and leap. Some fly, while a few glide. Some animals scarcely move at all!

Flying squirrels don't really fly. But they can glide, taking off from one tree to another. Their patagium—the membrane that looks like a wing—acts like a parachute and helps keep them in the air.

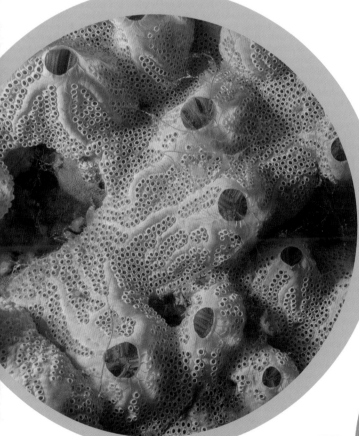

Sponges stay rooted in a single spot all their lives.

Jellyfish contract and relax the muscles in the top part of their body, the bell, to move. This forces out water in a jet behind them, which propels them forward.

Elephants may live most of their lives walking on land, but they can swim too!

Frogs can jump away from danger. Their bones, muscles, and joints have evolved to help them leap.

Humans are bipedal. We walk on two feet! Can you name other animals that are bipedal?

HOW FISH SWIM

Fish swim with their whole bodies. They move their bodies in a wave, bending back and forth, which propels them through the water. Their tail fin, or caudal fin, helps them move.

WHAT DO FINS DO?

Many fish use their fins to steer. Some fish use their pectoral fins–the first set of fins–to move. Other fish use them more as brakes, or to help maneuver quickly in tight spaces.

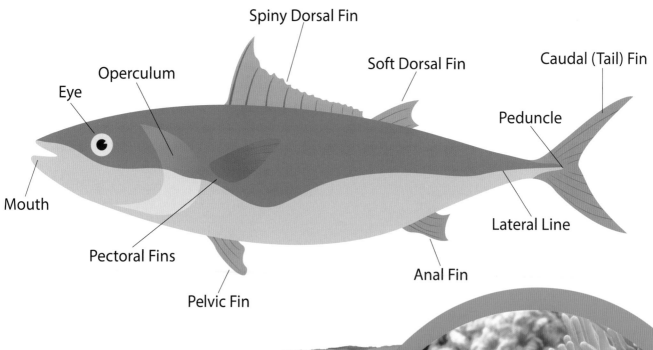

Spiny Dorsal Fin

Soft Dorsal Fin

Caudal (Tail) Fin

Operculum

Eye

Peduncle

Mouth

Lateral Line

Pectoral Fins

Anal Fin

Pelvic Fin

SWIM BLADDERS

While not all fish have a swim bladder–sharks, for example, do not–many do. A swim bladder is an organ that fills with gas and helps keep the fish buoyant in the water.

SWIM BLADDER

MATERIALS

- Sink
- Plastic bag that seals shut
- Penny

Step 1

Fill the sink with a few inches of water. Put a penny in the bag and seal it shut, without any air. Push it to the bottom of the sink. Then let go. The penny weighs down the bag and keeps it at least partially submerged in water.

Step 2

Take your bag out of the water. Open up one end, just a little, and blow into the bag to fill it with air. Seal it again.

Swim floaties that keep young kids buoyant in the water are acting like a fish's swim bladder.

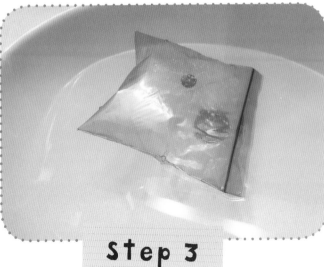

Step 3

Submerge it in water. Push it down to the bottom of the sink, then let go. It immediately pops to the surface.

HOW BIRDS FLY

The bodies of birds have evolved to help them get, and stay, in the air. They have light bones with a honeycomb structure, strong chest muscles, and a streamlined body.

WINGS

Birds' wings are shaped so that more air flows above the wing than below the wing. This helps create a force called lift that counters the force of gravity.

FEATHERS

What do a rhino's horn and a bird's feathers have in common? They are both made of a substance called keratin—you have some in your nails, too! Keratin is a tough, fibrous protein.

TAKING IT EASY

When a bird glides along without flapping its wings, it is using less energy.

BIRD-WATCHING

How many birds can you see in an hour?

MATERIALS

- Pen or pencil
- Notebook
- Binoculars (optional)
- Camera (optional)

Step 1

With the help of an adult, do a little bit of internet research on birds in your area. What birds can you expect to see at this time of year? What do they look like? Are any birds migrating through your area?

Step 2

Go to your backyard or a nearby park. If you live close to an arboretum or botanic garden, take a family trip.

Step 3

Sit relatively still for an hour or so, noting in your notebook which birds you see in the sky and whether you see any birds in trees near you.

HOW MANY BIRDS DO YOU SEE? CAN YOU IDENTIFY THEM?

DO YOU SEE A BIRD TAKE OFF INTO FLIGHT? HOW DO THEY MOVE THEIR WINGS AS THEY DO SO?

DO YOU SEE A BIRD SOARING ON AN AIR CURRENT?

DO SOME BIRDS SEEM TO FLAP THEIR WINGS MORE? DOES IT HAVE ANYTHING TO DO WITH SIZE?

COMMON NORTH AMERICAN BIRDS

Northern cardinals. The male is known for his bright red feathers.

Mourning dove. Its wings make a whistling noise when it takes off.

The starling was mentioned in William Shakespeare's *Henry IV.* Supposedly, a man who wanted to bring all the birds mentioned in Shakespeare to the United States imported them to Central Park in New York City, and they spread throughout the nation.

Maine and Massachusetts both claim the black-capped chickadee as their state bird.

Subspecies of the red-tailed hawk are found throughout North America, ranging from Canada to Mexico.

The American white pelican is one of the largest birds in North America.

The great horned owl has great night vision.

The male red-winged blackbird has the bright red wing that gives the species its name.

HOW ANIMALS STAY WARM

One way scientists classify animals is to say whether they are endothermic or ectothermic. In common terms, are they warm-blooded or cold-blooded?

Endotherms, or warm-blooded animals, are able to maintain a stable body temperature regardless of their environment. Mammals, including humans, are warm-blooded.

Some endotherms hibernate. Their metabolism slows down, and their body temperature drops. Arctic ground squirrels can have a body temperature close to freezing!

Ectotherms, or cold-blooded animals, are greatly affected by the temperature of the environment around them. Reptiles and amphibians are ectotherms. A reptile in the sun will have a higher body temperature than a reptile in the shade.

TAKE YOUR TEMPERATURE

Normal human temperatures are clustered around 98.6 degrees Fahrenheit, but they can fluctuate during the course of the day, and from person to person. What is your normal body temperature range?

MATERIALS

- Thermometer
- Paper
- Pencil

Step 1

Decide on three times that you will take your temperature every day for a week: one morning time, one afternoon time, and one evening time. You should not eat, drink, or exercise for a half hour before taking your temperature.

WHAT HAPPENS IF YOU TAKE IT AFTER DRINKING A HOT DRINK, OR A COOL ONE?

Step 2

On the first three days, take your temperature at the same three times and record the results. Is your temperature always the same? If not, when is it highest or lowest?

TAKE YOUR TEMPERATURE IMMEDIATELY AFTER EXERCISING FOR 20 MINUTES. DO YOU SEE A DIFFERENCE FROM A DAY YOU HADNT EXERCISED? WAIT A HALF HOUR AND TRY AGAIN.

Step 3

Once you have established a baseline, try experimenting with the afternoon or evening recording. What happens if you take your temperature right after eating a snack?

BLUBBER GLOVE

How do animals like whales, seals, and polar bears stay warm in cold water? Let's do an experiment to see.

MATERIALS

- 4 disposable vinyl gloves
- Ice
- Lard, butter, or shortening
- Large mixing bowl
- Stopwatch or phone with a stopwatch function

Step 1

Fill a bowl with ice.

Step 2

Put on a glove, and submerge your hand in the ice. Have a friend, sibling, or parent start the stopwatch when you put your hand in.

Step 3

Remove your hand when the cold becomes uncomfortable. How long did you last?

Step 4

Put on a fresh pair of gloves and find a source of kitchen fat. We used lard here.

Step 5

Spread the fat over one of your hands, coating the glove.

Step 6

Place a clean glove over that hand. You now have a layer of fat between the two gloves.

Step 7

Back your hand goes in the ice!

Step 8

How long can you last this time? We doubled our time, from 45 seconds to close to two minutes. The layer of fat keeps your hand warm.

WHAT DOES BLUBBER DO?

Mammals that live in cold water have a thick layer of fat called blubber underneath their skin that keeps them warm. Blubber can be several inches thick—even up to a foot thick! In the experiment, the lard, a source of fat, acted like blubber to keep your hand warm. But blubber helps in other ways, too. It stores energy and helps animals float. Pretty cool for a layer of fat!

Blubber isn't the only adaptation that polar bears have. Their short, thick claws help provide traction on the ice. A polar bear's fur is very thick, too. Its fur and blubber trap heat so well that bears are hard to spot with infrared cameras.

Emperor penguins have not only blubber, but lots of feathers—more per square inch than any other bird.

Beluga whales live in Arctic and sub-Arctic regions. Unlike many whales, they don't have dorsal fins on their backs, which helps them keep a streamlined profile under the ice. Their white skin helps them camouflage themselves.

Ringed seals have thick claws that help them maintain holes in the ice to let them breathe.

DNA

Why are your eyes the color they are? What determines the shape of your nose, the color of your hair, or whether you have an allergy? All these things are determined by your DNA. The cells in your body know how to function because they are getting instructions from your DNA.

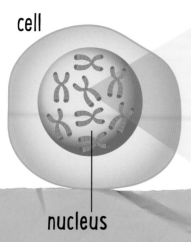

cell

nucleus

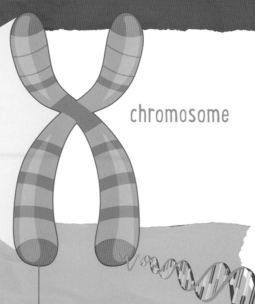

chromosome

telomere

DNA

DNA BASICS

- DNA stands for deoxyribonucleic acid.
- Every single cell of your body contains DNA.
- Humans aren't the only ones who have DNA. Every living thing has DNA.
- DNA is found within parts of your cells called chromosomes.
- Sections of DNA are called genes.

DNA
DEOXYRIBONUCLEIC ACID

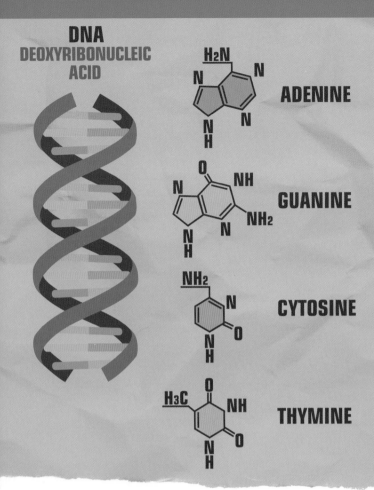

ADENINE

GUANINE

CYTOSINE

THYMINE

THE FOUR BASES

DNA is built from four nucleotides, or bases: adenine, thymine, guanine, and cytosine. DNA forms in a very specific structure called a double helix, which has been compared to a ladder twisted into a spiral. The rungs of the ladder are two bases paired together. Adenine and thymine always pair together. Likewise, guanine is always paired with cytosine. The order of the bases act like a code, telling cells what proteins they should make.

MUTATIONS

Sometimes, somewhere in a chain of DNA, there is a change or mistake. Maybe a base is left out, or an extra base is put in. Mutations can cause diseases, but they can sometimes be beneficial.

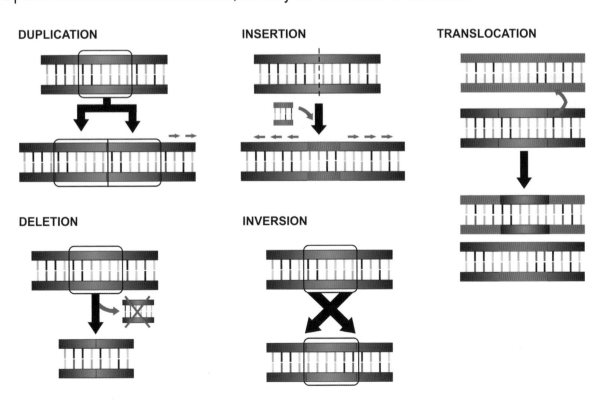

DUPLICATION

INSERTION

TRANSLOCATION

DELETION

INVERSION

DNA MODEL

Make a DNA model that looks like a twisted rope ladder, just like real DNA.

MATERIALS

- 4 different colored highlighters
- Colored tape (such as painter's tape)
- White paper
- Scratch paper
- Ruler
- Pencil with eraser
- Scissors

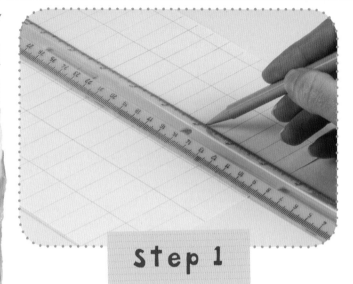

Step 1

Using a ruler and pencil, mark the white paper into about 25–30 strips, each ½ inch (1¼ cm) wide and 1¼ inches (3 cm) long.

Step 2

Cut out the strips with scissors. These strips are the rungs of the ladder. Each one represents a pair of chemicals known as bases. There are only four different bases in DNA. You will use a different color highlighter to represent each of the bases.

Step 3

Erase any stray pencil marks on the strips. Fold each strip in half so that it consists of two equal-sized rectangles. The crease marks the dividing line between two bases. In real DNA, the two bases in each rung are held together by a chemical bond.

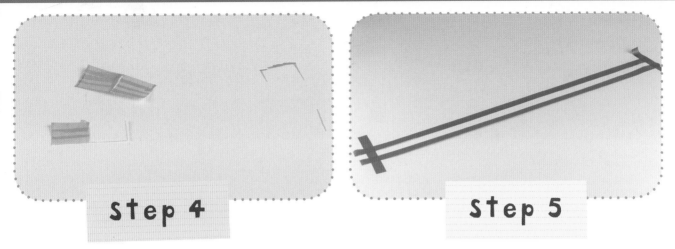

Step 4

Lay down scratch paper. Use 4 highlighter colors to represent the four bases in DNA. Color the paper strips so that one half is one color, the other half another. The colors should always be in pairs. For example, orange always goes with pink in our model. Color the strips identically front and back.

Step 5

Cut two strips of colored tape, each about 28 inches (70 cm) long, for the sides of the ladder. Lay them parallel to each other, sticky side up, with about ¾ inch (2 cm) between them. Use short pieces of tape to keep the two sides in place while you add the paper rungs.

Step 6

Press paper rungs (base pairs), in any order, onto the two lengths of tape, leaving a gap of about a ½ inch (1 cm) between the rungs of the ladder.

Step 7

When you've used all the rungs, carefully fold both lengths of sticky tape lengthwise. This will hold the rungs between the folded pieces of tape.

Step 8

Gently twist the ladder into a spiral shape that's just like DNA itself. You can tape one end down or have another person hold it and twist from the other end. *Can you see why DNA is described as a double helix?*

HOW DOES IT WORK?

DNA (deoxyribonucleic acid) is found in the cells of all living things. DNA holds coded instructions that control how people, animals, and plants look and function. The bases—as represented in your model—are a code of instructions for how to make proteins. Proteins are needed for the structure, function, and regulation of a person's tissues and organs. A section of DNA that carries a recipe for a particular protein is called a gene. Humans have about 20,000–25,000 genes.

BREATHING

All animals need oxygen. But different animals take in oxygen in different ways.

Fish breathe in water, then expel it through their gills. As water travels out through the gills, it leaves oxygen that sustains the body.

Mammals, including humans, have lungs. When humans go underwater, we hold our breath, storing oxygen in our lungs while we dive or swim. But some seals actually exhale before they dive. They store oxygen in their blood and muscles.

Insects don't breathe in through their mouths, or have lungs. Instead, they have little openings on their body called spiracles. Air enters through these spiracles and travels through the insect's body through tubes called tracheae. Then carbon dioxide is released as a waste product back through the spiracles.

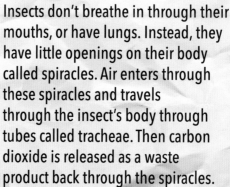

Some humans can hold their breath underwater for twenty minutes! That ability is rare, though. Most people can hold their breath for about two minutes.

YOUR LUNGS

Step 1

How many times do you inhale and exhale in a minute at rest? Set a timer for one minute and see how many times you inhale and exhale. Record that number.

Step 2

How does exercise affect your respiratory rate? Exercise for 20 minutes or so and then check how many times you inhale and exhale in a minute. It should be higher. Your body is working harder during exercise and needs more oxygen.

Step 3

Does age affect your respiratory rate? Check the respiratory rate (at rest) of the members of your household. See if they vary in any way.

Step 4

How long can you hold your breath? Take a big breath, start your stopwatch, and see!

Most adults breathe about 12 to 20 times a minute, faster during exercise. Most kids have a higher respiratory rate—a 10-year-old may breathe up to 30 times a minute, a toddler may breathe up to 40 times a minute, and a baby may breathe up to 60 times a minute!

HOW HANDS WORK

Human hands are amazingly versatile and useful. With them, we discover textures, detect heat and cold, pick up and put down objects, wave away insects, hold pencils and phones, and more. Our opposable thumbs are especially useful in helping us grasp objects.

Opposable thumbs are not very common in the animal world, but humans aren't the only animals to have them. A number of primates have them. So do pandas—they use a sixth toe to grasp bamboo.

Fingertips have a lot of nerves and touch receptors. They can distinguish sensations that other patches of skin cannot. To demonstrate this, close your eyes. Have a friend or parent do the following, but scrambling the order:

- Touch the end of a pencil or chopstick lightly to your back. Ask how many pencil(s) are touching you.
- Touch two pencils or chopsticks side by side to your back. Ask how many pencil(s) are touching you.
- Touch two pencils or chopsticks to your back, about an inch apart, then two inches apart, then three. Ask how many pencil(s) are touching you each time.

Do the same tests with your fingertip and your wrist. How far apart did objects need to be before they registered as separate objects?

ARTIFICIAL HAND

Build an artificial hand out of drinking straws and string to mimic the way a real hand works.

MATERIALS

- Pen or marker
- 5 plastic straws
- Cardstock
- Tape
- String or embroidery floss
- Scissors
- Pencil

Using a pencil, trace your hand onto a sheet of cardstock paper.

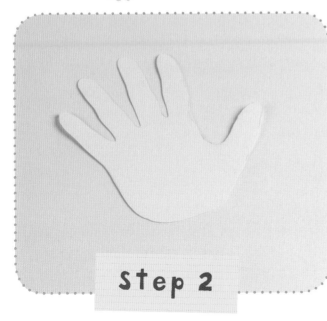

Cut out your hand with scissors.

Place your hand on the cutout and make pencil marks on either side of each joint. Joints are the places where fingers bend.

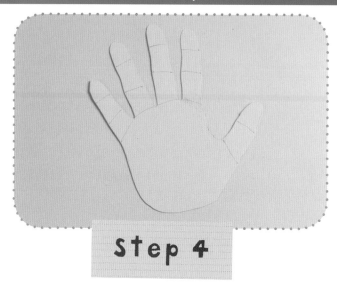

Step 4

Connect the pencil marks with lines where joints are located.

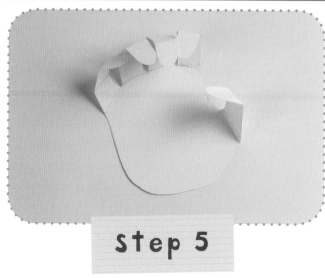

Step 5

Fold the fingers forward at each line.

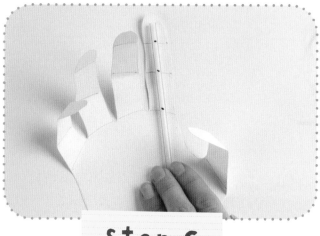

Step 6

Place a straw on top of a finger so that the top of the straw is a little below the top of the finger. With a marker or pen, mark the straw at each joint. Repeat for all other fingers.

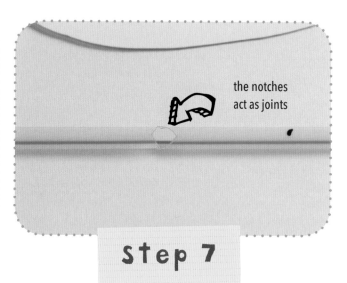

the notches act as joints

Step 7

Use scissors to cut a triangular notch from the front of the straw where you marked each joint. Don't cut all the way through the straw. Repeat for all other fingers.

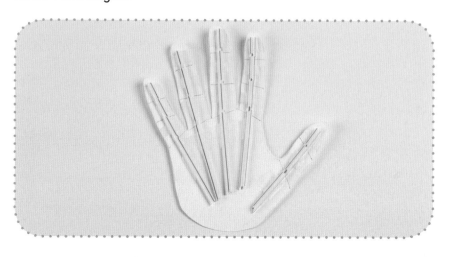

Step 8

Tape the straws down to the cardstock fingers so the notches line up with the fold lines. The cut-out notches should face up. Trim any excess straw length from the bottom. Straws should end in the palm area.

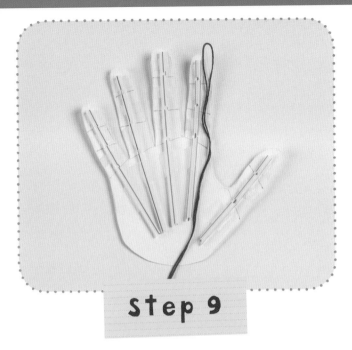

Step 9

Cut a piece of string or embroidery floss for each finger that is at least twice the length of the straw.

Step 10

Tie a double or triple knot at one end of the string. Thread the other end of the string through the top of the straw (the fingertip) and out the bottom (near the palm).

Step 11

Run the knotted end of the string up over the top of the fingertip and tape securely to the other side. Repeat for all fingers.

Step 12

Your artificial hand is now complete. *What happens when you pull the string at the bottom of a straw? Can you pull all strings at the same time? How is your artificial hand different from your real hand? How would you improve the design?*

HOW DOES IT WORK?

The human hand is an amazing work of engineering. It has five fingers that each have multiple joints. These joints are controlled by muscles and tendons. The muscles pull on the tendons, which pull on the joints and make them bend. Think about all of the ways your fingers bend. In your artificial hand, the notches in the straws act as the joints and the strings running through the straws act as the tendons.

FINGERPRINTS

Each person's fingerprints are unique. In investigations, a person might have their fingerprints tested to see if they are a match for fingerprints left at the crime scene. You can do a low tech version of dusting for fingerprints and recording them!

MATERIALS

- Clean glass
- A fine, powdery material such as flour or cocoa powder
- A brush
- Clear tape
- Dark paper
- White paper
- Pencil

Step 1

Press your finger against the clean glass to leave a fingerprint. It may help to rub your fingers together to bring oil to the surface. (You don't want to try this experiment right after washing your hands.)

Step 2

Hold the glass to the light to see if you've left a clear fingerprint. If not, try again.

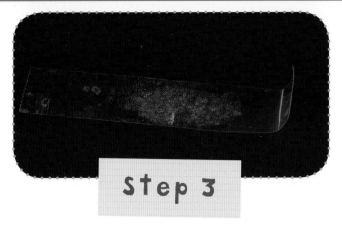

Step 3

Step 4

Use clear tape to "lift" the fingerprint from the glass. Press the tape to the glass, and remove it from the glass, slowly and carefully. It will be easiest to see against a dark background like black construction paper.

Now record your own fingerprint. Scribble a square on a paper with a pencil.

Step 5

Step 6

You'll end up with a lot of graphite on your finger!

Press a finger into the graphite left behind by the pencil.

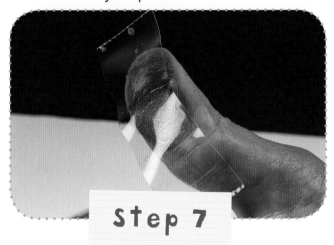

Step 7

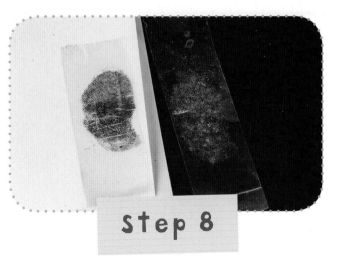

Step 8

Press tape against your finger and remove it. Perform this step slowly and carefully.

Compare the fingerprints lifted from an object against the fingerprints taken from graphite. Are they a match?

VISION

Vision varies tremendously in the animal world. Humans have binocular vision—each eye perceives an image, and our brain puts it together. If you close one eye, your depth perception can suffer. That is, it gets harder to figure out how far away something is.

Humans can see light in the visible spectrum. But some animals can see longer or shorter wavelengths than humans can.

WAVE LENGTH IN NANOMETER

700

600

580

550

475

450

400

RADIO WAVES

MICROWAVES

INFRARED

VISIBLE LIGHT

ULTRAVIOLET

X-RAYS

GAMMA RAYS

Bees can see lots of ultraviolet light that reflects off plants.

Some snakes can see into the infrared spectrum. This helps them detect warm-blooded prey around them.

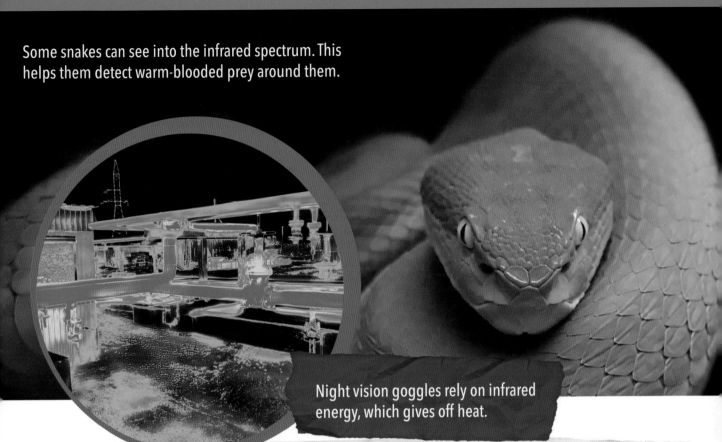

Night vision goggles rely on infrared energy, which gives off heat.

In humans, light enters the eyes through the pupil. The iris, the colored part of the eye, controls the size of the pupil and how much light gets into the eye. Light lands on the back of the eye, the retina, which has structures called rods and cones. Rods help us see in dim light, while cones help us see color. The optic nerve carries images to the brain for interpretation.

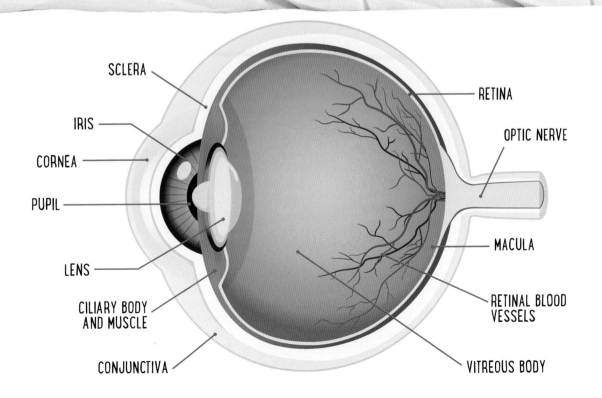

SCLERA

IRIS

CORNEA

PUPIL

LENS

CILIARY BODY
AND MUSCLE

CONJUNCTIVA

RETINA

OPTIC NERVE

MACULA

RETINAL BLOOD
VESSELS

VITREOUS BODY

CORNER OF YOUR EYE

You can see things around you without moving your head or your eyes! This is called peripheral vision. You can test the limits of this vision. It takes two people to do this activity, so grab a friend.

MATERIALS

- 1 black marker
- 4 other markers of different colors
- 5 index cards
- 6 popsicle sticks (pencils also work)
- Masking or painter's tape
- A table or desk
- A chair

Setting up:

1. On one index card, draw a small black dot.

2. Draw on each of the other cards a different shape in a different color.

3. Tape one card to each popsicle stick.

Experiment:

1. Sit at the table or desk. Hold the card with the black dot in one hand straight out in front of you.

2. Ask your friend to mix up the shape cards where you can't see.

3. Your friend puts one of the shape cards in your other hand without you looking at it.

4. Stare at the black dot in front of you. Keep your eyes on it the whole time. Do not move your head.

5. Hold the shape card straight out beside you. Slowly move it in an arc toward the black dot card. Remember: Don't look at it!

6. When you can see movement in the corner of your eye, stop your arm. Your friend puts a piece of tape on the table to mark that spot. Then continue slowly moving.

7. Stop so your friend can add a mark when you can tell what color the card is. Do the same for when you know what shape it is.

8. Do the same thing with the remaining three cards.

What do you see first?
Last?
How far does your peripheral vision go?

EXTRA CHALLENGE!

Switch hands. The moving hand now holds the black dot. Your other hand moves with a shape card.

OPTICAL ILLUSION

Sometimes, you can trick your eyes and your brain.

Line Lengths

Which line is longer—the horizontal line or the vertical line?

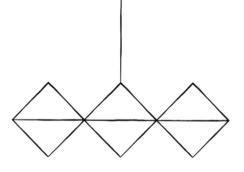

Heart and Soul

What color is the heart in each quadrant?

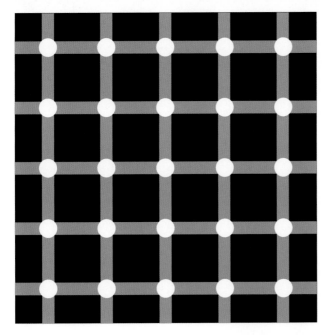

C

DECEPTIVE DOTS

If you let your eyes roam around this image, you're likely to experience a warping effect.

D

FLASHING DOTS

Stare at this grid long enough and the dots will flash on and off. Why?

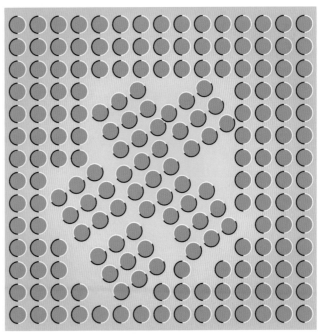

A. Though it may be hard to believe, the horizontal and vertical lines are equal length. The diamonds placed at the ends of the vertical line make it appear longer. The 3 diamonds laying over the horizontal line break this line. The interruption makes the combined parts seem shorter.

B. The pink hearts in the top right and bottom left squares are darker than the other 2 hearts, right? Wrong! All 4 hearts are identical in color. The lighter background color in the top right and bottom left squares make the pink hearts seem darker by contrast.

C. This is an afterimage illusion. The white dots look brighter because they are surrounded by a lot of black. This enhances the afterimage illusion, where an image of something stays in your eye even after you've looked away (like "seeing" a camera flash after it's already gone off).

D. This is known as anomalous motion, a term used to define the appearance of motion in a static image. Color contrasts and eye movement contribute to relative motion effects.

BLINKING

Blinking helps keep your eyes from getting dry. How often do you usually blink? How long can you go without blinking?

For this experiment, you'll need another person to help out, as well as a stopwatch or timer.

Step 1

Watch the other person for one minute. They should not try to keep from blinking, just blink naturally. How many times do they blink in one minute?

Step 2

Now, have that person watch you for one minute. How many times do you blink? Generally, people blink 10-15 times a minute, though they may blink less if they're concentrating on something.

Step 3

Run the experiment again. This time, try not to blink. How long can you keep from blinking?

Step 4

How long can the other person keep from blinking?

MONITORING THE WORLD

Today, we have a lot of ways to monitor our world. We can check a weather forecast to see what kind of clothes to wear, glance at a smartphone to see the time, and use a GPS to tell us how to get from one place to another. In the past, scientific instruments were simpler.

Most car dashboards show time and temperature.

AIR PRESSURE

We can't see the air, but that does not mean it doesn't have weight. Layers of air higher in Earth's atmosphere put pressure on the air layers closer to the Earth. As these areas of high or low pressure change or move, they affect the weather. Tools called barometers measure air pressure, which helps people make weather forecasts.

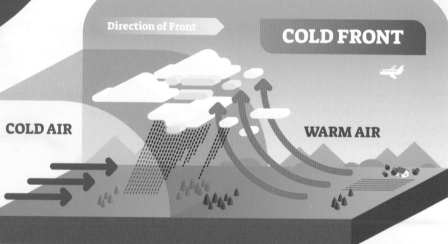

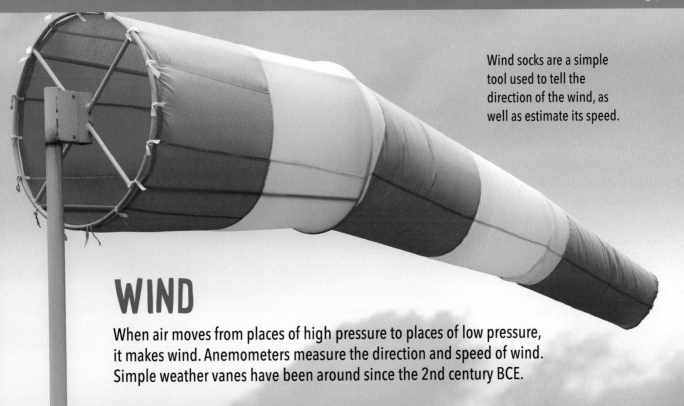

Wind socks are a simple tool used to tell the direction of the wind, as well as estimate its speed.

WIND

When air moves from places of high pressure to places of low pressure, it makes wind. Anemometers measure the direction and speed of wind. Simple weather vanes have been around since the 2nd century BCE.

TEMPERATURE

Where does the word Fahrenheit come from? Daniel Gabriel Fahrenheit (1686-1736) was a physicist and inventor who invented an accurate thermometer that used mercury. While thermometers had existed before that point, they weren't very reliable. In many other countries, and in scientific studies, people use the Celsius or centigrade scale to measure temperature. It is named after Anders Celsius (1701-1744), who was a Swedish astronomer and physicist.

HUMIDITY

If you're asked to think of water, you'll probably imagine its liquid form. But it's around in its solid form as ice, and it's present in the air in its gaseous form, water vapor. Hygrometers measure how humid the air is—that is, how much water vapor is in it.

WIND VANE

You can make a wind vane from simple materials you have at home.

MATERIALS

- 1 large plastic cup
- 4 small paper cups
- Gravel or small stones
- Glue
- Tape
- Scissors
- Straw
- Marker
- Ribbon spool
- Lightweight cardstock
- 4 craft sticks

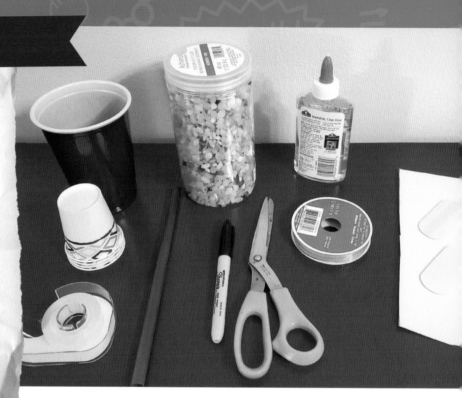

Step 1

Trace and cut out two cardboard circles the size of the top of the plastic cup.

Step 2

Fill the bottom of the plastic cup with gravel or small pebbles to weigh it down.

Step 3

Using the end of the scissors, poke a hole through the center of each cardboard circle. Each hole should easily allow the straw to pass through. Tape down one cardboard circle to the plastic cup with the straw in place.

Step 4

Secure the craft sticks to the second cardboard circle with glue and/or tape.

Step 5

Secure the four paper cups to the craft sticks with glue and/or tape. Draw on one to distinguish it from the others.

Step 6

Put the ribbon spool on top of the plastic cup. It acts as a turntable that allows the top of your wind vane to move smoothly.

Step 7

Place the top of your wind vane on the bottom cup. Make sure it spins freely. How many times does the marked cup spin by in a minute?

HOT AIR

Did you know that air expands when it is heated? The molecules move faster and further apart. This simple experiment illustrates that point.

MATERIALS

- Empty soda bottle
- Balloon
- Container of hot water

Step 1

Stretch out the empty balloon. Secure it on the end of the empty bottle.

Step 2

Place the bottle into the container of hot water. The balloon expands!

HOW DOES IT WORK?

When air is heated, the molecules inside move faster. They also move further apart. Hot air is less dense than cold air. When the plastic soda bottle conveys the heat from outside, the air inside the bottle expands. It has no place to go except into the balloon. As the water cools, or if you take it out, the balloon will deflate again. Thermometers with a thin tube of liquid inside, such as mercury, work on the same principle. The liquid expands as it gets hotter, rising in the tube.

BAROMETER

You can't measure exact air pressure with this homemade barometer, but you can measure a change in air pressure.

MATERIALS

- Jar
- Balloon
- Rubber band
- Straw
- Tape
- Ruler
- Construction paper or other sturdy paper
- Scissors
- Pen

Step 1

Cut off the bottom from a balloon.

Step 2

Fit the top of the balloon over the top of the jar.

Step 3

Secure it with a rubber band.

Step 4

Tape a straw to the top of the jar.

Step 5

Fold the paper in half. Draw lines at regular intervals on the sheet of paper.

Step 6

As the air pressure rises or falls, the straw will rise or fall as well. Place the jar in a place where the temperature will not change, as that will also affect the straw.

If you have a barometer, keep it next to your homemade barometer. Track changes in your own barometer and compare them to the actual one and the weather outside. How accurate is your barometer?

SUNDIAL

Before clocks, people marked the passage of time with sundials. Make your own!

MATERIALS

- Paper plate
- Marker
- Pencil
- Tape
- Watch

Step 1

Carefully poke a hole in the center of the plate.

Step 2

Place the plate on the ground, with the pencil standing upright. In a sundial, the object that casts the shadow (here the pencil) is called the gnomen.

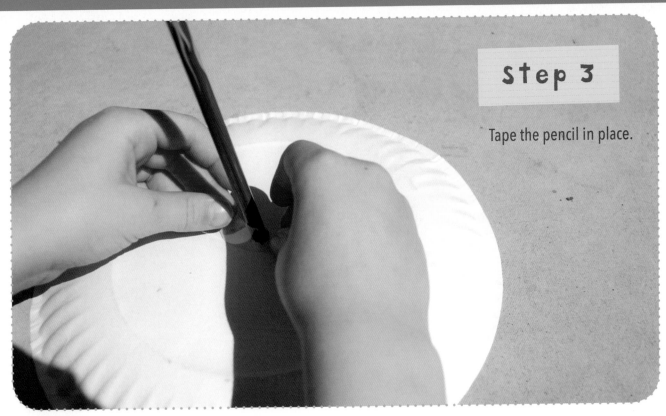

Step 3

Tape the pencil in place.

Step 4

As the day passes, the pencil casts its shadow in different places. Mark where the shadow falls and the time.

LATITUDE LOCATOR

If you look at a globe, you will see an overlay of imaginary lines. People use them to assign each place a set of geographic coordinates.

Latitudes

Earth Axis

Equator Line

Longitudes

The horizontal lines mark latitude. The equator is at 0 degrees, with the North Pole at 90 degrees North and the South Pole at 90 degrees South. The vertical lines mark longitude. Longitude marks the distance East or West from a line called the Prime Meridian.

Honolulo 157° 50′ W
Mexico City 99° 10′ W

Kingston 76° 48′ W

Barbados 59° 30′ W

Caracas 66° 56′ W

A plaque at the Royal Observatory in Greenwich, England; the Prime Meridian runs through the Observatory.

Rangoon 96°
Bangkok 100°
Saigon 106°
Addis Ababa
Bombay 72°

Each place on Earth can be defined by its geographic coordinates. For example, Chicago is found at 41.8781° N, 87.6298° W. New York is found at 40.7128° N, 74.0060° W.

You can find your latitude location with very simple tools—and the help of the North Star. The angle at which the North Star rises above the horizon corresponds to your latitude. At the equator, latitude 0 degrees, the North Star can be seen on the horizon. At the North Pole, latitude 90 degrees, you would have to look straight up to find the North Star.

MATERIALS

- Protractor
- Tape
- String
- A small weight
- Scissors
- Straw

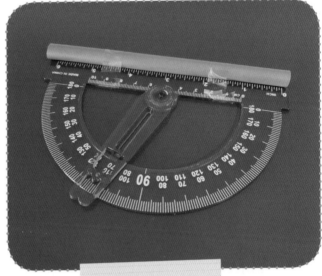

Step 1

Cut the straw to the length of the protractor and tape it on. This will act as a sight that will help you focus on the North Star.

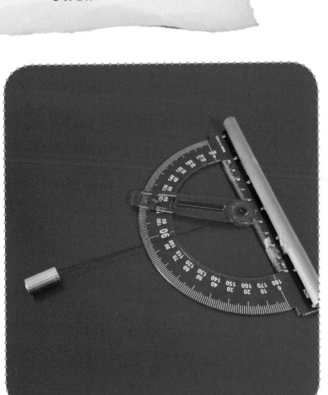

Step 2

Thread a string tied to a small weight through the small hole in the protractor.

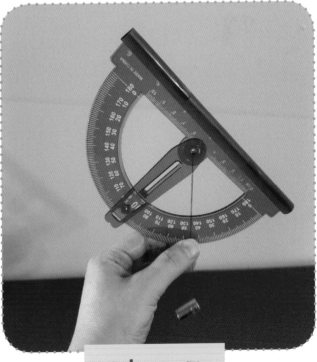

Step 3

The weight needs to hang freely.

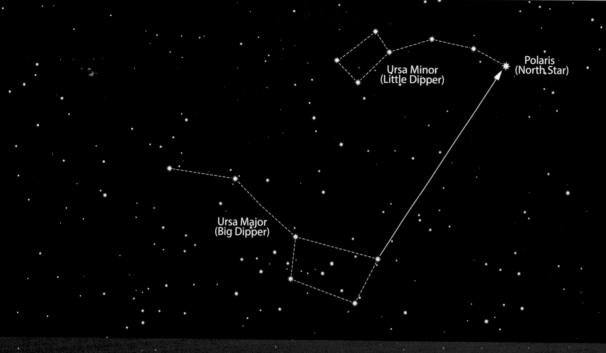

Ursa Minor
(Little Dipper)

Polaris
(North Star)

Ursa Major
(Big Dipper)

With an adult, go outside at night and find the North Star. Tilt the protractor up to peer at the North Star through the straw. Note where the string crosses the protractor.

The protractor has two lines of numbers: running from 0 at the side to 90 at the bottom, and running from 180 at the side to 90 at the bottom. At the equator, 0 degrees, if you were looking straight ahead at the North Star, your string would cross the 90 on the protractor. At the North Pole, 90 degrees North, you would have to tilt your protractor straight up, and the string would cross the 180 mark.

To get your latitude, just subtract 90 from the larger number and you have your latitude!

RAIN GAUGE

How much rain does your area get? Measure over time with this simple rain gauge.

MATERIALS

- Large bottle
- Small bottle
- Measuring cup
- Gravel or pebbles
- Scissors
- Ruler
- Tape

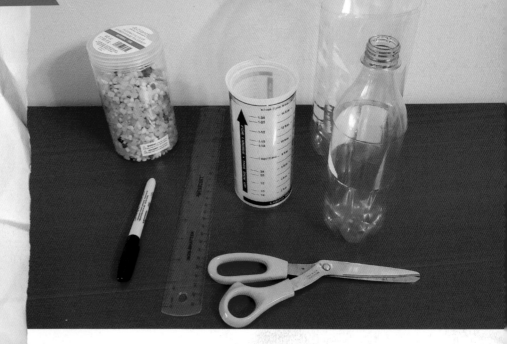

Step 1

Cut the tops off both bottles.

Step 2

Using the measuring cup, pour a quarter cup of water into the smaller bottle. Mark increments as you pour each half cup in.

Step 3

Add gravel to the bottom of the larger bottle to weigh down your rain gauge.

Step 4

Place the smaller bottle into the larger one.

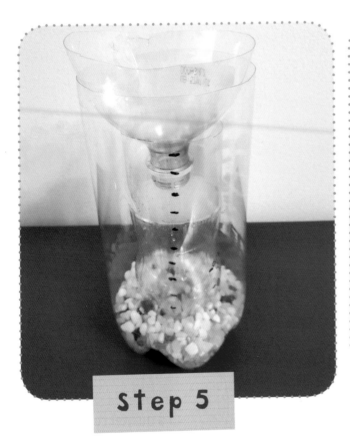

Step 5

Use the top of the larger bottle as a funnel.

Step 6

Tape the funnel into place to secure it. Place the rain gauge where it can gather water!